ON STONY )

On Stony Ground

GORDON MASON

PETERLOO POETS

First published in 2004
by Peterloo Poets
The Old Chapel, Sand Lane, Calstock, Cornwall PL18 9QX, U.K.

A catalogue record for this book is available
from the British Library

ISBN   1-904324-14-2

Printed in Great Britain by
Antony Rowe Ltd, Chippenham, Wilts.

ACKNOWLEDGEMENTS

Acknowledgements are due to the editors of the following magazines in which some of these poems, or versions of them, first appeared:

Borderlines, Candelabrum, Cencrastus, Cyphers, Envoi, Fife Lines, Flaming Arrows, Frogmore Papers, Honest Ulsterman, Orbis, Pennine Platform, Poetry Scotland, Poetry Wales, Prop, The Red Wheelbarrow, Smiths Knoll, Staple magazine, Understanding.

Thanks also to The Arts Council of England for a Writer's Award in 1999.

i.m.
Rachel "Bunty" Mason

Contents

Knapper says

The knack's
in the deftness –

kissing flint
just so

striking it hard
but not too hard.

Knapper says
the angle's everything,

that it's flaking gives
the stone its purpose –

hammer, scraper,
knife.

One look and he can tell
where an arrowhead is from:

some with as many faces
as a blackberry,

and they shine so too,
some, just bland, two-faced.

Stone doesn't come apart
like fish flesh does –

everything has to be
struck for.

And when he's finished,
each stone will have

the language its user
needs, each will have

kept its substance,
kept its silence.

Visitors to the Cathedral

Between John Lugg, 1645,
and William Hopwood, 1661,
there's a row of dots on the wooden,
commemorative-plaque signifying
the time when there was no organist,
when Cromwell's troops solemnly took
the instrument apart and paraded its
pipes through the streets of Exeter
like so many lifeless limbs cut from
the same cadaver.

Meanwhile, today, an elderly couple's
meditations are interrupted when the chair
one is sitting on collapses under him
sending the splintering sound echoing
high up into the cathedral's roof-space.
Attentive, volunteer staff help him to his
feet, comfort him, and replace the fabric
and beechwood chair with another one.

Missing organists, collapsing chairs –
minor breaches in the continuity, like
Cromwell's short-lived Commonwealth,
or the breath of kings.

But if you stand inside the West door where
the weak and infirm sat on stone seats
sculpted from the columns' base, so worn
they've had to be replaced with new Beer
stone, look East, and you can almost see
the trembling plumblines hanging in the air.

Verticals connecting earth to deep-space.
Deep-space and beyond.

11

The Mote

Moored all night in the loch of my eye,
it drifts on dreams, rocks in my slumber.

In the morning when I rub the sleep away
the stone skelf etches my eye, quick as a
skater's blade-figure-of-eight, bold graffiti.

Might have been a sand-fleck carried by
the wind as I crossed the sand-spit to
St. Ninian's isle: sand-shrapnel incising
its runes, its indecipherable ogham.

But neither the lotion I drizzle on the little
satin cushion in the corner of my eye, nor
the unstoppable wash of tears welling from
the duct, can assuage the pain or lift away
the frosted vision I am squinting through.

Some hope of an early release from this
Cyclop's head. Or comfort for a dreaming god.

The Specialist

I wanted to talk to you about diamonds:
how you select them, how you put them
together, pair them, sequence them,

above all what you see when you look
at them through your glass eye-piece,
turning them three hundred and sixty

degrees between finger and thumb,
rolling them back and forth on that
piece of black, velvet cloth. And what

it is like to be hunched-up hour after
hour with your inspection glass,
trapping and releasing light.

Looking directly at the sun.

Sticks and Stones

His name was Rutherford.
Rutherford had a round face
and a pudding-basin haircut.
I was afraid of Rutherford.
Rutherford was a bully.

Then came the new gym-teacher,
blond, some might say beautiful
in his elegant, navy leggings.
He introduced my class to boxing.
Put me in the ring with Rutherford.

I can still smell those leather gloves,
hear the boys shout – *Get 'im ! Get 'im*
but neither of us threw a single punch.

Rutherford stood in front of me bent-
double, hands over his ears, disappearing
somewhere fast into his own sweaty fear.
He was there for the taking.

Give 'im an uppercut ! Finish 'im!
they chanted. But Rutherford stood
stock-still waiting for the hammer-blow
he thought would come, knees long-
since turned to water, convinced that
I had surely acquired along with my
boxing-gloves the strength of Hercules
while his hands felt like lead.

And suddenly it was over.
Our teacher had intervened.

Head-down, Rutherford left the ring
unable to see through his tears, unable
to understand the boos which rang in
his ear were meant for me, not him.

I saw him, weeks later, by the fire-escape.
I noticed that under his fringe, he wore a
friendly smile. Gratitude perhaps?

Bite of my apple?

Schoolfriends

Of all of us, you were the nattiest one –
tailored suits, pressed shirts, polished
shoes, and such sleek and wavy hair.

You ballroom-danced a lot. And you were
the first to have it off with a married woman.
But that was it really – sex and good looks.

Bright too – we all thought we were in that
mediocre, post-war grammar-school for boys.
And the first to smoke. Sobranie Black Russian.

So how many women and how many wives
have you had in all the years since then.
And where are you now, such an enviable

handsome boy – the one we all looked for
in the mirror as we combed our hair to look
like you on Saturday nights, before the dance.

Knuckle-Stones

They came and went – the yo-yo, potato-gun,
French-knitting, diver-in-a-glass-of-water.

And I remember only a few of the moves in knuckle-
stones: *onesies, twosies, over-the bridge, through-*

the-gate, foursies – the one-shot sweep and snatch
as you tried to gather all the years and hold them

before your thrown-stone fell.

The Letter t

I form small letter t the way I do
because of Bob. I went to school with him.

He left early to join the Marines, and, after
Suez, came back only once.

We asked him how it had been, searching
his face the same way we did the boy who

claimed he'd gone *all the way*.
Bob was evasive. Quite unlike him really.

We'd been told he'd seen action. Hand-to-
hand. Egyptians killed. That kind of stuff.

But with each question we fired he withdrew,
sensing what it was we wanted to hear.

Time passed. Each went his separate way.

I form small letter t the way I do
because of Bob. I do it the way he did.

And sometimes, in my mind, I see him do it –
how he'd drop the letter's vertical then cross it

by running the pen back up the letter's spine,
and, moments before it reached the top, he'd

let it curve away. Bob's *pulled-shot* I called it.
His harmless ricochet.

Stanley's Folk

Stripped of guile, they go about
their business – wringing clothes,
dusting shelves, scrubbing floors,
busy even at their resurrection.

Heaven and Hell, I think, are really
just where we left them: rising from
our sleep, on the landing, wherever
it is easy to trip over them.

Long-Barrows on the Moon

Hard to find you, though Burials Office
(Leisure and Recreational Services) gave us
precise directions: *Section E, layer 200*.
We buried you there some thirty years ago

in a grave containing your younger sister,
and two infants, but all the paths had been
filled-in to save on maintenance, so the grid
I needed to find you had also disappeared.

A village cemetery, high on the hill then,
a road leading up to it as burial-places
have since neolithic times, like the cursus
I stood on last week leading to the barrows

on Thickthorn Down. That too, changed.
Now there are planted fields where once
a six-mile processional road of gleaming
chalk had been, where light from the rising

moon had illuminated all our ancestors.
Section E, layer 200. And I thought of
the bones in the county museum dug
from a Neolithic grave on Maiden Castle:

two infants, head-to-toe, looking as though
they'd just been put to bed – *Ian, Ernest Combes:
d. 21st September 1956, aged 28 days, Graham
Combes: d. 26th August 1959, aged 2 days.*

Leaving, I noticed the grave-keeper's cottage,
boarded-up. Another saving no doubt, like
the outside-tap that didn't work either. But we'd
found you in the end. Just where we left you.

Then home by motorway. And, high in a clear,
November sky, distinct as they sometimes are,
long-barrows on the moon.

Writing Chrysanthemums

For some it's drink, others it's chrysanthemums.
For others again, it's writing poetry.

Take them or leave them, they're all obsessions.
So no apology for writing this chrysanthemum.

Any way, you have your obsessions too – that
solar eclipse last year, and last night's lunar one

followed by tedious explanations of the relative
position of each planet, how its shadow falls

across another's path, and, of course (how could
I forget) the importance of the prevailing weather...

In the face of that, what could I do but assume
an identical orbit, manoeuvre your heavenly body

next to mine and dock in your landing-bay with
such finesse it earned prolonged applause from

ground-control (a neighbour's crackling radio).
Then, drunk on love, we lay and scanned the sky's

black water, watched as its myriad stars began to
blossom into white chrysanthemums. Then your

voice coming through the ether – *Everything will be
ok as long as nothing gets between us and the moon.*

The Sewing-box

(for Sarah)

Something has to be sewn back on,
caught before it gets any worse, made
whole, made fit, made ready.

But you catch the edge of the sewing-
box when you lift it off the shelf and its
contents spill across the floor – there's

a button you recognise but not where
from, a heap of needles fused like brilliant
spillikins daring you to pick them up.

It's your anger, though, surprises you,
as if the past had opened up to reveal
what you'd rather it wouldn't – the box's

quilted lining perhaps, like a little empty
coffin. And then, as if it were the most
obvious thing in the world, someone

hands you a magnet, and *hey presto!*
the needles are back in the tin again.
But it refuses to go away this memory

of accident or loss, so that when you
put the box back on the shelf and turn
towards the window, you can't help but

notice how the setting sun had started
to cast long shadows, and how the daisies
are covering their faces with pale fingers.

Ever the One

for bringing things indoors, mainly dead things, or
things with a echo of life still in them – a martin's tiny,
brown-flecked shell, a blackbird's, pure sky-blue.

Once, when we pulled the fingers of honeysuckle off a
wall, we found what you called a *seethe* of garden snails.
You wondered why you'd never seen baby snails before.

It was you who would find a still-born chick, spatchcocked
on the paving-slab, or a drunken fledgling, head too heavy,
loitering outside the kitchen.

In time you tired of them – the sea-shells, the beetles,
the bird or mouse's pure-white skull, the butterfly's half-wing.
Your interest waned. And, finally, you left.

Years later I found a matchbox in your room, inside a moth,
its body still intact but paper light and shut and secret.
I searched its feathery mask for eyes, but its camouflage too

good, I couldn't find them, so I returned it to the matchbox
and the matchbox to the shelf with all the other treasures
you'd collected, postponing the clear-out to another time.

But as I closed the door behind me, and saw the Midas prints
my finger left, gold-dust from your precious moth's wing, I felt
the moment fracture like a bird's egg. No more, no less a thing.

Terracotta Warriors

Miners up from the coal-face, leaving the lift-cage.

Coal-dust can taste as sweet as sugar you know.
But mostly it gets in the way of what I wanted to say.

Not a new phenomenon. I'll have the boiled potatoes.
They're soft and white. Unlike coal, whose heart is hard.

Funny thing though, some of it you can ease apart
with just your thumbs, like china-clay. Coal that is.

Or potatoes. Not hearts. So. Will they uncover us like
terracotta warriors who've been buried for centuries.

And how will we be, do you think. Upright.
On strike perhaps. Facing forwards, resolute.

Don't make a whole life out of a single sentence
you said, closing me down like a coal-mine.

Slieve Na Calliagh

(Hill of the Witch)

At the heart of the tomb my chatty, student
guide pointed out tri-spirals in the roof.

Then, because of my accent, said *I lived in*
London once. Couldn't tell one season from

another or night from day! By the way, you'll
find more markings on the satellite-graves outside

and behind them you'll find The Hag's Chair.
It has a cross engraved on the top from when

it was used in penal times. (Only if witches are
young and have ringlets down to their shoulders

could I possibly believe in them, I thought,
turning away as she welcomed more visitors)

So. Did they worship their ancestors, these people,
or the sun and the moon. And what do tri-spirals mean:

Birth, Love and Death, some kind of map, or just
what they saw after a few magic mushrooms.

Either way, they knew where to site their tombs.
Perhaps it's simple as that. A quality of place.

The right light. The right silence. High enough
to take your breath away. To remind you.

So that's what witches do – make you answer
the question you came to ask.

Sadly, when I turned to wave goodbye, she'd gone,
back into her grave no doubt. And I'd wanted to tell her,

still do, how just being there that day she'd given
the place some meaning. Turning night into day.

Freeing light from the stone.

Grimes Graves

We sink shafts.
We mine each other.

We forget how easy it is
to get lost in the dark, to

trespass where there are
no signposts, to take what

we want and leave the rest,
how easy it is to disclaim

what we leave behind: a ring,
an artifact, a small, clay figurine –

was this a pregnant woman?
Or how easy it is when we've

finished to fill the shaft up
with spoil from the new one,

sometimes forgetting to erect
that crucial notice: DANGER

DISUSED-WORKINGS.

At Peace

A pair of flightless angels with blind grey eyes
hovering above his tombstone reveal the slender

waists and shapely legs of women, our deceased
might think, though his inscription reads simply:

SERVED IN THE MAORI CAMPAIGN IN NEW
ZEALAND AS MUSKETRY INSTRUCTOR AND
ADJUTANT 12TH OF FOOT. AT THE CURRAGH
CAMP AS BRIGADE MAJOR. AND AS DEPUTY
ASSISTANT QUARTER-MASTER GENERAL AT
JHELUM IN THE FIRST AFGHAN WAR.

Altogether a fine man you would have thought.
And maybe he was, though his guardian angel's

book looks firmly closed on the matter.
He would have rued, I think, the killing of civilians –

would have felt it was like boxers leaving the ring
and going for the audience. No honour in that.

No honour in selling his medals in a car-boot sale.

And what would blind old women want with them anyway.

Sheelagh Na Gig

It is my lot to be stuck up here in
front of the whole parish holding
my fanny wide open, and my bare
tits hanging down to the waist.

Now, as far as I know, there are no
representatives of men holding their
cocks up the air say, as a warning
against the sins of flesh.

That, apparently, is a woman's job.
After all, was it not Eve in the first
place who corrupted Adam that balmy
day in the Garden of Eden. Well fine,

but I'd argue myself that both sexes
are perfectly capable of seduction.
What I can't fathom is why us poor
Sheelaghs have to be carved in stone

and placed above the portal of some
church for the whole of eternity. Oh,
and by the way, I have seen them,
your husbands and your boys, and

they do not, may God forgive them,
so much as lower an eyebrow when
they enter the portal of this church.
For all the good I am doing.

Broch of Gurness

*(Suddenly, the leg of his stool sank clear through the earth. That was earlier this
century. Then the site was opened up like the chest-cavity of a corpse and the grave-
goods examined. Later, a trust took over and re-arranged the site so tourists could peer
in, gasp outwardly, be inwardly bored, make connections, or make none at all)*

There we were with daylight all but
gone when we reached the car-park.

The wooden café lights were out.
There was a cold wind off the sea.

Everything returning to its own:
coaches turning out of the car-park,

shadows thickening under the trees,
the stillness of stones.

We hardly spoke as we drove away.
Instead, we watched as the stars

scroll up the windscreen, the field-
walls, caught in our headlights, being

reclaimed by the darkness behind us.

We had wanted to make a go of it.
Knew each other well enough, talked

it through many times, but always
something turned us, like the needle

to Magnetic North, to some deeper
personal history of our own, to some

burial-site where the grave-goods lay.

The Quarry

A bite out of the hill.
Or an apple.

Prams, fridges,
sometimes a body gets left

among the buddleias, nettles,
and rosebay willow-herb.

Maybe it's god I half-expect
to find here, hanging like a

black, plastic-bag from
the safety-wire, or lying

among the fist sized
stones to-hand.

Only the unclaimed dead
have the right to be here.

Under the scent of the lilac tree.
On stony ground.

Graveside

Now that today and tomorrow
have rolled into one, and the past,
not to be outdone by time and its
tricks of the trade, has come to your
graveside too, what shall we do?

What shall we put on your stone
now the earth has sunk and all that
we knew, that we recognised as you,
has shrunk to the bone, now that your
heart's gone too, what shall we do?

We could render you: *Devoted wife.*
Devoted mother. Sadly missed by
her sister and brother. We could.
And it would be true. But where
are the words that would do?

The stone-mason asked what stone
we wanted – ogee, half-ogee, polished,
part-polished, which lettering: roman,
block, or script. Did we want it cut-raised,
cut-flushed, painted or gilt.

Now that you've gone what shall we do,
when what we wanted to say went with you too?

Violets and Sorrel

You, at the worked-out gold-mine picking sorrel,
and chewing its bitter leaves. Me, the prospector,

panning for violets. Yes it's the same waterfall
that parachuted down when you and the children,

naked, wet-faced, screamed at the rising mist, and
still hysterical when you put them to bed, spilled

through your arms like eels into water, the kitchen
knee-deep in shorts and vests, and strewn across

the table our discarded flowers – violets, buttercups,
and bitter sorrel. On the floor a fan of golden grass.

Under the Hill

Sheep, at nightfall, stand knee-deep in mist.
Some make confession at a dry stone wall.
Others stand rooted, under the hill.

Sometimes they scatter like strewn marbles.
Sometimes, hypnotized by conformity, they
follow each other aimlessly in single-file.

Yesterday, I saw three buzzards hanging
in the air above them wing-tip to wing-tip,
a perfectly balanced mobile.

I was out when you called.
It wasn't 'til later I got your message
... *and don't forget the song inside yourself.*

So today I have been gathering hazel nuts,
still wrapped in their bright-green leaf-twists.
I am looking for the seed inside. Its milky song.

Silhouette

(i.m. Jonathan Mason)

An Autumn break down caves
to see what prehistoric painters
left behind – bison mainly, but
also deer and cows and horses.

A pastoral people – not a single
image of war among them, just
these elegant drawings of what
had been the utterly familiar.

Then, at Quercy, we come across
a hand-print: yellow ochre blown
through a reed across the artist's
hand as he held it against the wall.

A signature of sorts. A statement.
Like the silent one the boy left after
only five short days. A silhouette.
A hand-print. *I was here.*

Free-Fall

A clatter in the sky.

Ricochets and sling-shots.

Crows have no vowels,
only these consonants honed
to a sharp edge, only the oaths
they learn on high-rise estates.

But if I were falling, I would like
to be like them – black umbrellas
turning inside-out, somehow,
miraculously, righting themselves.

I would like to come out of this
plummet just like that – reaching
for the hyphen-bar one of them
has swung across the void to me.

Grottes De Villars

(Sites et Monuments)

A long drive. A hot sun.
Then a door in the hillside.

Behind the bone-yellow curtain
of calcite hanging from the roof,
the paintings looked much smaller
than we both expected: a small, blue
pony in mid-stride, and a stick-man
thrusting his belly out at a bison –
an early toreador. Elsewhere the claw-
marks of a bear, and a scoop mark in
the floor where generations settled
down to hibernate.

Back at the farm, we ate al fresco.
Talked 'til the darkness drove us in.

The next day we drove past sunflowers,
tall as Masai warriors, cows in a meadow
nose to nose like bison chewing the cud.
Manganese-oxide and a little animal fat,
you said, *and I could paint the walls at*
home with those two!

Time and silence. The critical fusion.

Krakow

All that was left was cabbage
and sausage in a thin gravy.

The *white wine* we asked for
turned out to be Russian sherry.

But when you arrive late and tired,
in the coldest of weathers, you eat.

No matter you consider you have
an educated palate.

A barn of a restaurant then:
tables in long rows end-to-end

a few other diners, mainly men,
mainly solo, scattered here and

there below the restaurant's near-
cathedral roof. Evidently the heating

for the day, the restaurant's quota,
had long ago run out.

To one side of us, a solemn diner
on his own was ordering vodka

two glasses at a time and swiftly
slapping them down his throat until,

and his waiter was ready for this,
he toppled slowly and stiffly side-

ways into the aisle between tables.
Then, with all the grace and timing

of a dancer, his waiter caught him
in a single elegant movement,

righted him, and then returned him
to his seat, just as you might return

a favourite book to its proper place
among the library shelves.

We paid in US dollars. Though we
wondered as we left whether hard

currency alone could keep a toppling
state upright, when the cold air hit it.

The Mountain

They all went into the mountain,
the best and the worst of them.
Some arrived alone, like the poet

and the painter, others arrived in
hordes still wearing prison uniforms
or the striped pyjamas of the camps.

Deeper and deeper they went,
driven by stories they had heard
or the stories their own minds had

conjured, each one clinging to his
dream, his vision of what lay at
the heart of the mountain – what it

might look like, what it might mean.
True, there were some, who after
everything, were still sceptical, had

only a blurred idea of the secrets
the mountain held at its centre –
the lake, the source, the spring.

And it was true. Everything they
had hoped for. Limbs became whole.
Minds became whole. The dead were

returned to them. Families were re-
united. And because it is in the nature
of man, they stood on the mountain

and happily spread the good news.
They sang and they shouted. They
sang and they shouted over the fields

and over the cities. But, because it is
also in the nature of man, no-one could
hear them. No-one was listening.

Millenium Stones

A buzzard I disturb has torn one side
of a rabbit's head clean off.

You can see the brain quite clearly.
It won't return, the buzzard, even after I've gone.

It will simply move elsewhere.
Kill something else.

Half-way across a field of rape I glimpse
two deer, their noses sharp as pencils.

When I approach they trampoline off-stage in fear.
And the circle of stones, when I find them, are lying

on their backs asleep, or listening to the hill breathe.
They are like corpses at some execution's aftermath –

what follows the *coded warning*.

Tonight the Moon

You remember the first moon-landings–
two exuberant Americans announcing
portentously, without a whiff of irony –

The Eagle has landed.

You remember the space-suits – inflated,
silver, acrylic party-wear, their moon-
buggy, straight off a Californian beach.

You remember that purposely inclusive
One small step for Mankind– so biblical
so pioneer they might have formed a circle

had there been more of them. They may yet.

Back here on Earth – a Dorset hill-fort
built by a Celtic tribe against the day their
look-out sees the Roman fleet, catches

the sullen light off breastplates, standards.
Senatus Populusque Romanus. Sling-shot v
artillery. No contest. *The Eagle has landed.*

Tonight, the moon. A cenotaph. A tomb.
Across its face clouds drift like tumbleweed.
The moon tonight. Last Chance saloon.

Bigamist

In the confusion, they left him for dead.
Pulled him from a heap of corpses and
brought him prisoner-of-war to a farm
in Wales. And there he was. Out of it.

Anyway, seems he met this girl at a local
dance, married her and had two children.
Girl and a boy. I'm one of them. The girl.
But nothing lasts forever.

I found out when he died he'd been writing
to another daughter in Germany all through
the war, and after. You know in what became
East Germany. Her mother was very bitter.

When my mother died, I decided to write a
few letters of my own. I'd found this German
daughter's address in the letters he'd been
receiving all through the war and after.

So we met. Liked each other straight away.
I said it was a bit of a jigsaw-puzzle same
father. Know what she said? Said we were
like fragments of a fallen wall. I liked that.

Standing Stones

Seeing the Helstone there
at the foot of a Dorset hill,
I thought of *the sliding craig*

at the side of the road outside our
village in Scotland. It had been
a helter-skelter for generations.

In the moonlight its surface
shone like polished leather –
even the diagonal cracks like

lines on the palm of your hand
were worn so smooth your body
could scarcely feel them, and no

matter that you started upright
still you ended up on your back
the sky unscrolling above you.

Most descended feet-first.
The bravest plunged down headlong.
Me. I am still falling.

Silverfish

An eat-anything-left kind of insect – wee
squirts of mercury at the back of the sink
like thoughts you had but couldn't get hold of.

Like the octopus, they don't waste a thing –
all that useful blue-black. (There is so much
love in the reservoir of a fountain-pen)

Their fishy tail helps – it gets them about in all
that wetness, like mud-skippers on a river-bank.
Elsewhere, they make a living in the binding of

old books in and out the pages like usherettes
at a cinema. Just like burglars, they're happy
with anything they can get their hands on.

Then vanish when you put the light on.

The Bug that Lives Below the Downstairs-Lavatory Outflow Pipe

We call our downstairs-lavatory
The Ice-box. The only heat is from
an infra-red bulb that warms the top
of the head but doesn't reach the cold

air winding round each leg. So I sit
and think of Africa. I think of India.
I think of anywhere that doesn't know
the chilling cold of an English Winter:

those fingers of fog, those frozen pipes,
the speechless mould on the window-sill
following some microscopic purpose of
its own. I think of Doultons, Twyfords,

Armitage-Shanks (such English names)
performing their essential duties to a far-
flung empire, and still no call from your
hospital, hot and far away as Africa.

So I contemplate the bug that lives
below our downstairs-lavatory outflow
pipe-head and thorax thin as a violin,
each slender antenna conducting its own

separate orchestra. I imagine it speaking
Xhosa– the clicks it makes like a telephone
returning softly to its cradle. The message:
Out of theatre. And she is doing fine.

When you get back, I want to tell you
about the constellation of blood-red stars
that came and went at the back of our
living-room chimney. I want to show you

the bug that lives below the downstairs
lavatory-outflow pipe. I want to take you
by the hand and lead you back to me.
I want to brush your long, dark hair.

The Definite Article

A necklace of small, brick houses strung
across a hillside, a Methodist chapel, a
corner shop that smelt of firelighters and
Wintergreen and Cox's Orange Pippins,

An infant school with BOYS picked out
above one door, GIRLS above the other:
memories of chancing the gap in the play-
ground wall which could lead the unwary

to sudden abduction and a good duffing-
up by the girls. Memories, too, of visits:
that missionary with his slides of Africa
far out-shining the Christmas-decorations

we made with our teacher. Then adolescence –
the lens that makes everything seem small,
bringing such a longing to be far away from
school and corner-shop and chapel and

further still from spelling, sums, extractions
by the travelling dentist – spitting blood in
holes in the playground dirt we'd made for
playing marbles. But if would be some years

before I came across the girl whose scent
would bring a close to my continuous present,
the simple mention of whose name would
break the necklace of the past.

The Slate Mine

Torrents of assonance and skitterings. Rafts of shale
that covered the entrance in a buckled sea of slate.

All Summer and Winter the chimney-smoke rises
that same slate-grey as the houses, trees and sky.

No-one looks up – but one-word greetings get
passed like betting-slips under the breath.

In the dusty silence of The Municipal Library
the unemployed read cover-to-cover, opening 'til

closing time: *The Theory of Flight, The Wonder
of Modern Prosthetics, The Life and Death of*

Atahualpa, and *How to Breed Whippets Successfully*.
Up at the mine the information-board warns you of

PERYL, instructs you – you stand at the entrance to:
A Museum Containing Implements In The Extraction

*Of Slate, Its Transportation By Railway To Portmadog
And Its Shipment Overseas*. A mine with a stomach as

big as a whale that could swallow men whole, grind
flesh, split femur, crush lung, and decapitate with

alarming precision. A mine that could make a widow
in the blink of an eye, a mine whose only light was

the one you wore on your helmet or the one that barely
flickered inside your head as the doctor patiently

explained the wonder of modern prosthetics.

The Burials

Summer, two thousand years ago, and someone's
put a sprig of milfoil at her head and, by her side, we
found charred bones – a child's some eight years old.
There would have been a little leather bag to hold these
poignant keepsakes, but it has long-since disappeared.

Whose past is it anyway. Not just hers I think:
our dead belong to us in a way the living can't.
That milfoil though – a cure for melancholy perhaps,
a footnote from the family to tell us how she died.

Elsewhere, another grave contains a man, some nineteen
years of age, a woman, thirty plus, her baby by her side.
*That the adults arms are pinned together by a wooden
stake suggests adultery. All three deaths are by suffocation.*

Or making the dead belong to us in a way the living can't.

Choker-Stone

We enter the cave like bats:
eyesight off, radar on, and

halfway in – about a mile –
a choker-stone has fallen

from the roof and blocks
the way, like words stuck

in the throat, or the heart.
Now only touch can be of

any help – that, and the little
echo sounds we make.

What else is there to do
but run our fingers over

one another's face, body,
hands: here an escarpment,

and there, the shipless
ocean of tranquillity.

Inside the moment I'm
clumsy as an astronaut

blind as a clothes-peg and
love, the unspoken word,

is the choker stone.

Sunset Canyon

(Long shot: a solitary rider,
flanked by massive walls,
makes his way up Sunset Canyon)

No hostile Indians, no mountain-lions
hiding in the rocks above his head, no
bounty-hunter's rifle glinting in the sun,
no vultures, rattle-snakes, gangs of wanted

desperados. No horseless stage-coach,
burnt-out wagon train, no camp-fire recently
abandoned, no tell tale tracks, watering-hole,
miner's shack, silent piano, frontier saloon.

No food, no water left, his horse gone lame,
his solitary role defunct, no way forward, no
way back, no tombstone raised against the sky,
no wooden cross, no hand-carved board –

Here lies a stranger who died from the heat, or a
broken heart. He left no horse, no name, no part.

Coming Up for Air

The brink. The one you don't know
if the water will be sacramental, cool,
or burn and thrill like whisky.

I remember the first time – her not
showing if she cared inside that cool
persona, feigning not to look where

I was standing on another platform,
out of earshot. And always those
unknown destinations. I could either

end-up drowning in those eyes, or
simply looking down the barrel of
her words. But always it's too late –

the train is taking her away with all
the others who will never know,
even as they step into the rain,

even as their lovers rush to greet them,
how much I fell in love with them.
Half-man. Half-seal. Coming up for air.

The Valley of Rocks

Heavy rain, sleet,
then snow.

Giant snow-flakes
dis-articulating

on the windscreen
and your mind

travelling back to
meeting your two

grown-up children
coming out of the sky

over India, back to
The Valley of Rocks

where all of us felt,
but no-one said:

Sometimes
you have to be like a rock

to survive,
you have to lie quite still,

render to the sky
what belongs to the sky.

Like the moon over India,
A giant snow-flake.

The Mill of Chaos

I'd brought the rain in my head of course,
just as I'd brought the missing sunshine.

Then, suddenly, the lake, as dark and shiny as a
grand piano. Huelgoat. A town besieged by forest.

There are some places, the Somerset Levels is one,
where something essential seems to be missing;

some void that threatens to tip the balance,
find its counterpart in you and suck you in.

Nothing daunted, we took the footpath round
lorry-high, glacial boulders choking the entrance,

past cataracts of lies and rumour – the turbulent
coils of water feeding The Mill of Chaos, and

further in, we found the rock our guide-book said
would tremble if we put our shoulder to it.

And it surely did. Still everything seemed poised
on some precarious edge. Almost. About to.

I think you brought that with you, you said,
knowingly. And you were right. After all,

God-forsaken, like chaos, is only in the head.

Abracadabra

We made love. We travelled together.
But now a postcard clinches what
we both already knew: you write

the wheel has turned full circle.

Living separately, keeping our
distance from each other, we had
thought to proof ourselves against

what happens when two people get
too close. But keeping the doors
between us locked was false security,

and now the end has come, your words–
the wheel has turned full circle, like
abracadabra, have unpicked the lock.

Questions

A bend in the river, and a Charolais bull
like a pi-sign, squat as a dolmen.

Downstairs, the Trinitarian abbey
convalescent-home to wounded Crusaders,

is puzzling the tourists with its terrible silence.
Next door, a shop sells lineage to Americans.

Why not. We all need roots. Or we think we do.
But the morning I saw that sitting hare get up

and take to its heels, I knew it is was over.
The morning I stumbled across that badger's sett,

big as an underground car-park, I knew I'd have
questions to face – like why did I come back

when I knew it meant pain for the two of us,
and why, when my mind is in lunar eclipse, do I

stalk the Winter fields we used to walk. And why
does truth have to lie in the ground for so long.

Long Lane

A stream and its debris:
blue fertiliser bags, a
cooker, a folding chair.

Here at the bridge folk
lose unwanted possessions.
Sometimes each other.

The stream, for its part, has
no choice but to plunge
beneath the road here.

Long Lane no choice but
to start its journey.
A bridge, a stream, a lane –

an intersection my memory
returns to, sifting for motive,
reason, blame, hoping for

the one essential clue that
solves the crime. You. Me.
Long Lane. Open verdict.

My Friend the Social-worker from Minsk

Saints Boris and Gleb are all of six feet tall
but only a few inches wide as depicted by
Russian monks on their fifteenth-century
icons: Russian as Red Square, or Moscow's
frozen river, or The Kremlin covered in snow,
transformed today into the Portobello Road
on a cold and golden evening.

As is the way, our conversation lights on
work, the balancing-act your job demands
(Whose side are you on anyway). But this
is your home-ground, and Minsk, it could
have been Odessa, only the place where it
started, where maternal grandparents with
bundles of belongings took flight to the West.

Two generations later and your patch covers
the entire White City estates and Hammersmith
as far as the West London Synagogue which
you didn't attend either – all that stuff dumped
long ago with Boris and Gleb, and all the saints
and corpses that one day turn up under the ice.

As we turn down Westbourne Grove, your small,
tired voice is like the flickering of a candle.
It says: *This is what I do. This is where I belong.*

Moon Walk

They left behind a colour photograph
where colour had never been and,
underneath the space-craft, a dance
of footprints from their moon boots
like herring-bones in a sea of dust.

Truth is, everything gets smutty up
there on the moon – even the Imperial
flag on the astronaut's knapsack ended
up covered in dust.

Back then, we were all moon-struck,
naïve. And now we're the experts in
highjacking moons, have been since
the day that colour photograph – an
astronaut and family – fell upwards
to the moon.

Terrace

Small brick houses,
redder and more silent
than the underwater corals.

A family's little tragedies
unfold behind these doors.
And then the house is sold

and others come to suffer loss
and know some happiness.
Easy to imagine its narrow

hallway, open door. Easy
to feel its silence vibrate
inside, its atoms hum.

Breaking and Entering

The A5 into Wales. Llangollen. Corwen.
Row after row of orthodox sheep at prayer
against the dry-stone walls.

Sometimes we enter each other's country,
each other's minds without so much as a
by-your-leave, or so I thought as I neared

your house near the worked-out mine, frozen
streams of slate like grey-blue lava. And now,
you wrote, you've reached your own A5:

ROAD CLOSED. DIVERSION. MARRIAGE OVER.
After all the years together, there really wasn't
too much left you said – each of you living off

each other's borrowed capital. So much for love,
I thought as I approached your open door, not
at all sure why I really came.

If you look someone straight in the eye,
I heard someone say, you can see their reality.
But it has to be straight in the eye.

Rain Moving in from the West

During the storm that was yesterday
the sea dumped logs of water on
the beach and, far out, fathoms deep,
an orchestra drummed and rolled.

In the calm that was afterwards, I
came across a scatter of cuttlefish-
bones, white as a dead man's hand,
dry and colourless as truth.

Also, I found a single translucent,
plastic sandal like the skeleton foot
of someone you feel you once knew
but whose name you can't remember.

But why am I wandering the beach
like this. I should be demonstrating
against global-warming, the arms-race,
or any number of tyrannical regimes,

I should be searching for God or Buddha,
falling in or out of love and writing
the appropriate poem, instead I am
thinking of my grandmother: how

she'd comb my hair with a fine-tooth
comb searching for head-lice eggs,
how she'd wash it in green-lye soap,
then towel it dry against her breast

as if I had just come out of the sea.
Sandals and cuttlefish. Memories and
mermaids. And behind each poem,
the burglar-proof hills.

Land's End

What if I said I'd meet you here at Land's End's rock-
strewn moor, its mason's yard of broken stones,
its litter of abandoned starts.

What would its chambered cairns, its bronze-age field-walls,
quoits and fogous, the finger chimneys of its disused tin-mines
(those headless, surreal flowers of brick and stone) tell you.

Here, the rain comes straight in from America.
It sweeps round standing-stones – *Blind Fiddler, Merry Maidens.*
It drowns *The Giant's Grave,* and breaks on *Doctor Syntax' Head.*

The air, the air is full of ghosts. Look to it, you wreckers. Look to it.

P.O.W.

(England 1944)

Not shunned so much
as barely noticed.

Everything about the farm
was out-of-bounds, *verboten*.

Only the shitty cattle, cattle-yard,
and milking-shed allowed,

so was it wise to arm them
scythe and sickle in the Spring

folk said, or let them join us
at the village hall to watch

the weekly film in silence
at the back, and she,

the sickly one of four who
wouldn't, come what may,

reveal the one she'd gone with
to the quiet fields of celandine,

nor knew that silver seeds
like thistledown were falling

from the sky all over Europe too.

The Enemy

When the heroes
of small kindnesses
become *the enemy*
its men wear striped
unbuttoned shirts,
its women, the cotton
headscarf of despair,
its children, only
the dark brown eyes
they stand up in.

Judas

Far too caught up with it. Way out of his depth.
He'd be first to admit it. But he's got a job, working nights.

And he's joined a group who meet to pray, every Sunday.
They pray a lot, he says.
But at least he's among folk he can trust.

Looking back, he says he was very young at the time.
Says he was easily led, with no intention of trying for history's jackpot.
Claims he forgot to fill-in the *no publicity* box.

But the memory's still there. He admits that.
Though he says he's learned to see it *out there* as if it wasn't 'his'
memory,
Learned that from another group.

But he'd like to find a cure for the migraines, and the psoriasis.
Funny how everyone who meets him mentions exactly the same things:
those strange, cerulean-blue eyes, and how pre-occupied he looks.

How was it someone put it.
Like a man who was trying to find himself.

Lava

Outside, a cracked, blue-rhino skin.
Inside, a python's carmine entrails.

No vertebrae. No legs.
Its columns pour forth.

Well. That was how you liked to see yourself.
Irresistible. Unstoppable as lava.

But then your ardour cooled
and what you'd wanted left unattained.

Then everything slowed to a standstill,
like the warm, rubber wheels of a bus

as it comes to a halt at the kerbside.
I really didn't know what to say to your parents.

Except of course you were quite beautiful;
beautiful as a sculpture in a sculpture park.

Though I still can't find a way to explain
the frozen smile. Your pose. Lot's wife.

Middle America

A row of houses stalled at the edge of town
like a train that's waiting to enter the station.

At the traffic-lights, the engine of a car, whose
driver is contemplating adultery, ticks over.

The driver is chewing at syllables.
Should he. Shouldn't he. Amber. Green.

By mid-day the sky is down to its shirt-sleeves.
Redemption is running late.

Pavane

Here we go, drifting across the sky
hand-in-hand: Earth, Venus, Mars.
This is the way we cross the universe –
hermaphroditic stars light years apart
as if there was all the time in the world.

Then there were those who lived in
Sniper's Alley – stringing up blankets,
running pell-mell behind the dancing
cloths to fetch a loaf of bread, making
love, or being burnt in cellars.

Nine months on, and just when we'd
forgotten what it was to lie and watch
the planet's slow pavane, they broke,
the waters of the moon, and from
the cellar of the sky a dancing child,
Earth by name. Venus, out of Mars

Summer Air-Show

First butterflies, more at the mercy of flight
than in control of it, looping and bucking
on updraughts of air, somehow managing
to rise on their carnival, dope-paper wings.

Then came beetles in their flying-machines
Dover to Calais, straight as you go, Orville
Wright and Bleriot. We clapped every one,
even though we couldn't see the pilots' faces.

After that came moths in petrol-engine
bi-planes. Erratic. Kamikaze. Intent on self-
destruction or so it seemed as they dived
towards the flaming barrels on the runway.

Then, as the light began to fade, high up,
returning to base, a squadron of crows.
Dorniers and droning Blenheims. We
counted them in under a darkening sky.

Before we left, dive bombing each other
with our plastic showground windmills
(red, white and blue of course) and just
when we thought it was over, suddenly

the night sky filled with parachutes – a
thousand flares that hung like glittering
snowflakes, irridescent may-bugs, or a
silent drift of stars arcing across the sky.

When it was over, we felt the chill on our
cheeks, that earthy softness under foot,
the damp smell of mud and wet grass.
It was a long way home with no wings.

Love in December

By four o'clock daylight has
ticked away, the trees stand-
to for a minute's silence.

Your letter arrived today.
The envelope was cold.

Strange how we think we've
said what we wanted to say
only to find we haven't.

So I'm shuffling the words again.
Here. Choose one. Any one.
What does it say?

Granular Matter

I'm giving you the choice
Just say you've finished with me!

I thought I knew what she meant,
but the possible meanings shifted
inside my head like sand: she might
have meant she wanted him to have
the guts to say it was over, the anger
in her voice anticipating all the pain
of her shattered pride.

But his silence said it all. It was over,
though he wouldn't say it. Wouldn't
let her make him say it. Was that it?
Why she bullied him, daring him to
hurt her – hurting him before he could her,
taking his choice away, making it hers –

I'm giving you the choice!

Overheard moments. Sand in the hour-
glass. Solid, granular. Granular, liquid.
Liquid, granular. Granular, hard.

Icebergs

Aeons ago, we rose from the sea.
Our polar lungs unstrung a syntax.
Look was the name traveller gave us.
Pity – a word without meaning.

Each day the penguins skittle each other
senseless in their rubber wet-suits,
the wings of the albatross unpleat the sky.
As for us, we have nothing to say to each other.
We will melt without ever knowing the meaning of love.

Suicide

You enter the sea fully-clothed, and the cold
of it freezes your legs. It gives you a headache.

No matter how she left – spinning on her heel
or weeping at the door whose handle she's never
had such difficulty turning, the fact of it is bigger
than who is to blame.

Somehow, though, you know she won't be back.
Any more than you will walk out further, catching sight
of what shoes look like underwater, for the very first time.

Brighton Beach at Midnight

We sat among the pebbles:
the faces of all the people
we have ever known.

We laid our hands on them
and felt their warmth
come through our skin.

Meanwhile, out at sea,
The Big Wheel turned,
shedding its light in droplets

like the stars that fall on water.
Palace Pier. A steamer
making for the moon.

Outward Passage

The boy sitting next to me
in the ferry terminal's nicotine-
brown waiting room gnawed

the quick of his finger then
removed it to assess the damage –
what meat was left on the bone.

Dun Laoghaire behind us.
A mild, October night.
And the sun slotting down

behind the Wicklow mountains.
From where you were standing
watching the boat's streaming wake,

you slowly turned yourself to face me
and formed the moment just: *Suppose
it was for the very last time, this.*

Holy Isle

A whale, basking in the sound,
its back out of the water.

Crossing to the island-monastery
won't be easy: two seas meet here

one form the East, one from the West,
and the water in the middle

rises like the hackles of a dog.

In the past they'd have crossed
in a wooden craft,

gone to sit out the distance,
see things as they really are

then upped and died or simply
abandoned Eynhallow, the Holy Isle.

The last tram standing at the terminus.

Primal

Today I was thinking of magma that
superheated stone, unstoppable as sex,
insistent as hunger, primal as fear.

Today I was thinking of sunlight
warming the earth, driving the winds,
heating the soil, rousing the seed

fueling the flower. I was also thinking
how after a storm the grass bounces back
of its own accord. How it gets up on its

own two feet so to speak, smelling of babies
and sporting an outrageous, punk hairdo.
Then I thought – how can I possibly account

for all this, except that we are only one of many
shrinking meteors balling their way through space.

Everything Into Reverse

Even as the Ladies' Flower Club,
St. Magnus' cathedral, Kirkwall,
holds its annual competition,
brokers in the London Stock Exchange
tear their tickets into artifical snow
for cleaners to remove at close of play.

So who's to say what's pointless
and what is not I thought as I
entered the exercise-yard of a
down-town shopping mall, itself
no less hermetic than St.Magnus'
Kirkwall, or the House of Commons.

Everything into reverse.
Upside-down. Inside-out.
What price the little dipper then
who, underwater, walks upstream
in search of food, who, unawares,
turns hunger into miracle.

After the Snow

I thought when the curtain came down,
and the heroine stepped up for applause

that the look on her face lay somewhere
between the tragic role she'd played

and her own reality. I also thought,
stepping out into daylight, how lucky

it is there's a hand either side you can hold
which eases you back inside yourself,

otherwise you might be left there stranded
in that other world, quite unready for the next.

Touchstones

I have been askin' myself of late
what it might be that would improve
this great democracy of ours, what in
the light of our growin' self-knowledge,
we might need to alter in our historic
Constitution, and I have come up with
the notion that we are more than
singularly concerned with our right
to *the pursuit of happiness.*

For some time now I have noticed
how much our appetites have grown.
I only recently remarked how,
the more we try to satisfy them,
the more insatiable they become,
and how the number of those whose
aim it is to stoke those appetites
has also immeasurably increased,
as has their reward for so doin'.

Instead of measurin' a man's worth
by his possessions and his ability
to acquire them, I concluded that
it might be provident if we found
a new set of touchstones against
which to measure ourselves.

Suppose, for instance, we declared
that, among the inalienable rights
we so wish to defend, we also
enshrined certain inescapable duties,
and that one such duty might be
the obligation of each and every
one of us to live our lives driven

by mutual reciprocity. It would
seem a man might still retain his
right to *the pursuit of happiness*
but that his happiness might indeed
be the greater for carin' about others
as well as himself.

I respectfully present all this for your
consideration, Mr President, and trust,
for the sake of our great nation, you will
address its concerns sooner rather and later.

Brick-Dust

(for I.H.)

Just a note to say thank-you for lending me your cottage.
Your neighbour waved everyday as though she'd won the lottery!
And did you know a mouse has taken up residence at the back of
the fire-place: that little pile of brick-dust outside the hole is a
dead give-away. Can't say I've seen him, but I have this fellow-
feeling for him – the two of us together, me writing poems,
him excavating the brickwork. Up at the farm, the Buddhist group
is no doubt doing something similar.

Then, last night, as I lay and watched the moon slide its silver coin
        through
a slot in the clouds, I thought – I must get in touch with everyone soon,
show them the brick-dust on my fingers. Tell them I love them.